Published by Creative Education
123 South Broad Street, Mankato, Minnesota 56001

Creative Education is an imprint of The Creative Company.
Design by Stephanie Blumenthal
Production design by The Design Lab
Art direction by Rita Marshall

Photographs by Alamy (POPPERPHOTO), Corbis (NOGUES ALAIN/CORBIS SYGMA,
Andy Warhol Foundation, BBC, Bettmann, Jerry Cooke, Julio Donoso/CORBIS
SYGMA, ROBERT ERIC/CORBIS SYGMA, Hulton–Deutsch Collection, Pawel Libera,
Thierry Orban/CORBIS SYGMA, SUNSET BOULEVARD/CORBIS SYGMA, Selwyn
Tait/CORBIS SYGMA, Pierre Vauthey/CORBIS SYGMA, FORESTIER YVES/CORBIS
SYGMA) Getty Images (Hecht/Pix Inc./Time Life Pictures), Frederick Warren

RUDOLF

Excerpt from *Nureyev* by Rudolf Nureyev, copyright © 1962 by Opera Mundi, Inc.
Used by permission of Dutton, a division of Penguin Group (USA) Inc. /
Interview with Rudolf Nureyev by John Gruen, excerpted from the *New York
Times*, June 21, 1970. Reprinted by permission of John Gruen.

Library of Congress Cataloging-in-Publication Data

Fandel, Jennifer.
Rudolf Nureyev / by Jennifer Fandel.
p. cm. — (Xtraordinary artists)
ISBN 1-58341-380-4
1. Nureyev, Rudolf, 1938–1993. 2. Ballet dancers—Russia (Federation)—Biography—
Juvenile literature. 3. Choreographers—Russia (Federation)—Biography—Juvenile
literature. I. Title. II. Series.

GV1785.N8F36 2005
792.8'092—dc22   2004063412

First edition

2 4 6 8 9 7 5 3 1

XTRAORDINARY ARTISTS

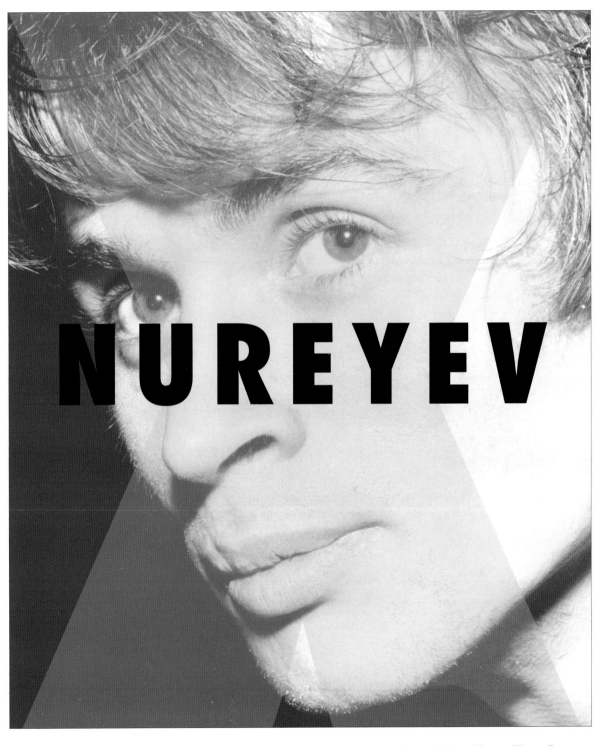

NUREYEV

JENNIFER FANDEL

CREATIVE EDUCATION

ON A NOVEMBER NIGHT IN 1958, FLOWERS RAINED DOWN UPON THE KIROV BALLET STAGE AS RUDOLF NUREYEV DANCED. NEVER IN PEOPLE'S MEMORY HAD A BALLET BEEN STOPPED TO CLEAR FLOWERS FROM THE STAGE—AND FOR A DANSEUR, RATHER THAN A BALLERINA, AT THAT. FROM THAT NIGHT ON, FLOWERS WERE BANNED AT THE KIROV, BUT THERE WAS NO STOPPING RUDOLF'S DEVOTED FANS. NIGHT AFTER NIGHT, THE FLOWERS FELL. FROM HIS FIRST YEARS AS A PROFESSIONAL DANCER, ADMIRERS AND CRITICS ALIKE WERE MESMERIZED BY RUDOLF'S REVOLUTIONARY TALENT AND EMOTIONAL PRESENCE ON THE STAGE. WITH HIS LIMITLESS ENERGY, TEMPESTUOUS PERSONALITY, AND AMAZING VERSATILITY, RUDOLF NUREYEV BROUGHT THE MALE DANCER'S ROLE INTO THE SPOTLIGHT LIKE NEVER BEFORE, TRANSFORMING TRADITIONAL BALLET FOREVER.

Rudolf Nureyev was born on a train shuttling eastward across Russia. It was

March 17, 1938, and his pregnant mother and three sisters were traveling to the coastal town of Vladivostok, where Rudolf's military father was stationed. Rudolf's mother was happy to finally be able to present her husband with a son.

Rudolf's parents, Farida and Hamet, both came from peasant families around Ufa, a town south of the Ural Mountains. To them, Russia's newly established Communist Party offered hope of rising from their humble beginnings. Hamet joined the Communist effort as a soldier and *poltrouk*, one who educated fellow soldiers in Russian history.

During World War II, as Hamet fought near Moscow in western Russia, five-year-old Rudolf and his family moved back to Ufa. They lived in an *izba*, a one-room wooden shanty with a dirt floor, with two other families and survived on an endless diet of pota-

Nureyev and his longtime dance partner Margot Fonteyn were often showered with flowers, as here, after a 1965 performance of Romeo and Juliet

toes. At desperate times, Farida sold their possessions, including Hamet's civilian clothes, to feed her family. But there was one thing Farida would never sell: their family radio. From an early age, music sustained Rudolf, transporting him from their cold, bleak existence to another world.

Rudolf began school at the age of seven. Barefoot and dressed in his sisters' hand-me-down clothes, he was called "beggar" by his fellow classmates. The taunting and laughter filled Rudolf with shame at his family's poverty, and he withdrew into himself. Still, he was delighted by school and the class's lessons in folk dancing. Whether at home or school, this new discovery—dance—alleviated his loneliness.

That same year, Rudolf experienced his first ballet. Although his mother had only

"Ballet was never easy for Rudolf. He had to work terribly hard for what he had. And he was willing to sweat blood for it."

— *Georgina Parkinson, British ballerina and fellow Royal Ballet dancer*

one ticket to a performance in Ufa, she brought her four children, and when a rowdy crowd pushed its way into the ballet house, the family followed. Once inside, Rudolf drank in the splendor of the theater, from its crystal chandeliers to its velvet seats and curtains, and fell in love with the dancers' graceful movements. Years later, Rudolf recalled of the experience, "Watching the dancers that night, I had the absolute certitude I was born to dance."

From then on, Rudolf devoted himself to folk dancing and gained a reputation in Ufa as "the boy who dances." Unfortunately, his father did not share in Rudolf's pleasure

when he returned home from the military. Convinced that his son should be fishing and hunting instead, he beat the eight-year-old and called him "Ballerina," the same name his fellow students used to tease him.

Despite this discouragement, Rudolf continued to dance. At age 11, he met 70-year-old Anna Udeltsova, an Ufa woman who had danced professionally. Udeltsova gave the boy free lessons, training him in the basics of ballet—plies, battements, and the five positions—twice a week. Rudolf's instructor and townspeople who recognized his talent were heard to say, "He should go to Leningrad," the home of the famous Leningrad Ballet

School. But his family's low income made even the train ticket there an impossibility.

Around the age of 14, Rudolf worked his way up to a position in the Ufa Opera Ballet. After volunteering as a stagehand, he was hired to perform small roles as a walk-on. The next year, the director hired Rudolf as a member of the corps de ballet, where he received his first professional training. Yet when offered a full-time position, Rudolf turned it down. In his head still rang the words, "You should go to Leningrad."

Rudolf at last found his way out of Ufa at age 17. When the lead dancer for the Ufa Opera Ballet missed his audition for a nation-wide dance exhibition in Moscow, Rudolf

volunteered to replace him. The teenager's performance earned him a ticket to Moscow, bringing him so near to Leningrad that it seemed only a breath away.

After performing in Moscow, Rudolf splurged on a one-way ticket to Leningrad. Arriving at the famous ballet school, the hopeful dancer introduced himself to the director, saying, "I am Rudolf Nureyev from the Ufa Opera, and I want to study here." The director was impressed by the bold, unflinching words of the waifish young man standing before him. For Rudolf, there was only the future. He had nothing to lose.

In 1955, Rudolf was accepted into the Leningrad Ballet School, where many great masters of Russian ballet—including Pavlova, Nijinsky, and Balanchine—had studied. After Rudolf's entrance audition, the examiner said, "Young man, you'll either become a brilliant dancer or a total failure. And most likely you'll be a failure!" The examiner saw passion and instinct in Rudolf's dancing, but, at age 17, Rudolf was entering the school six years behind most other students. Most dance instructors believed that training must begin at a very young age in order to develop the necessary flexibility, strength, and stamina. A start as late as Rudolf's was practically unheard of.

Rudolf found life at ballet school grueling and painfully regimented. Preferring his own tattered clothes to the school uniform, he was quickly branded a misfit. Rudolf slept through his math and science classes and went out each night to hear classical concerts and watch ballets, sometimes without notifying his superiors.

Because Rudolf started so late with his training, the school's director, Valentin Chelchov, placed him in grade six (of nine total grades), even though he was much older than his fellow classmates. In an effort to tame the young dancer and quell his rebelliousness, Chelchov humiliated him daily, calling him an "idiot" and a "provincial good-for-nothing." The director also placed Rudolf so far back in the class that he scraped the wall when he danced, wearing his tights thin. One day, after Rudolf was caught sneaking out

Nureyev was much older than most students entering the Leningrad Ballet School, who typically began their training at the age of 10

at night, the student and director exchanged heated words. Frustrated by Rudolf's lack of discipline, Chelchov transferred the teenager to the eighth grade and instructor Alexander Pushkin, convinced he was setting him up for failure.

Pushkin was a patient instructor who resisted the urge to correct Rudolf's unorthodox form and instead allowed him to discover his own technique. For months, Rudolf struggled to make progress while fellow students treated him like an incompetent outsider. But to Rudolf, his classmates were lifeless dancers with no spark of originality. Their techniques may have been perfect, but there was no emotional intensity fueling their dancing. Rudolf was sure that's what made him different—and better—than them.

Pushkin encouraged Rudolf to remain in his ninth-grade class for two years to ensure that his skills were fully developed. In Rudolf's last year of training, Pushkin allowed him to choose his own ballets to study, and he was given the lead roles in nine full-length ballets performed for the public. Rudolf also danced in the National Classical Ballet Contest in Moscow, where he received his first big break. Impressed by his performance, the three best ballet companies in Russia—the Bolshoi, the Stanislavsky, and the Kirov—each offered him top positions as a full-time soloist.

ballet was an important part of culture life in Russia, where people
revered the art and made national heroes of its stars

15

Rudolf began his professional career as a soloist with Leningrad's renowned Kirov Ballet at age 20, after only three years of professional study. From the moment he took the stage, people in the audience could be heard whispering to each other excitedly. This strikingly handsome dancer with the wide cheekbones, full lips, and dramatic eyes expressed each ballet's emotions not only with his face, but his whole being. Ballet aficionados were hooked, and their gaze fixated on the star danseur rather than the prima ballerina. In one of his earliest performances, Rudolf overheard a female usher exclaim, "When this boy dances, he doesn't know where the earth or the sky is." Instead of throwing roses to the ballerina, female fans tossed giant peonies onto the stage for Rudolf.

Rudolf's sudden popularity caused jealousy in the company, as he was given freedoms not bestowed on his fellow dancers. He was allowed to revise choreography, and he modified his costumes to visually lengthen his rather small build, baring his chest and doing away with the modest bloomers Russian danseurs wore over their tights. But what galled fellow dancers the most was Rudolf's behavior. When things didn't go his way, he often threw tantrums, swore at fellow dancers, and walked out of practices. To Rudolf, such behaviors were justified in the name of passion. Dancing was the most sacred thing in his life, and he grew irritated with fellow dancers who treated their work like a sterile office job. He believed, as he said throughout his career, that "every step must be sprayed with your blood."

"Rudi's driving force throughout his career . . . was to make up for the lost years of early training. To my mind, much of his eruptions and tantrums derived from a deep-seated anxiety and frustration, his insatiable desire to perform, to be on stage . . . to overcome the 'lost years.'"

— *South American ballerina Nadia Nerina*

In 1961, while Rudolf performed on tour with the Kirov Ballet in Paris, newspapers raved about the 23-year-old star, referring to him as the Kirov's "cosmonaut" for the new direction he was taking traditional Russian ballet. Reporters also enjoyed chronicling Rudolf's exploits around Paris. While fellow dancers explored the city from their tour bus, Rudolf went off on his own, making new French friends, sightseeing, and partying at clubs and discotheques. Toward the end of the Paris tour, the Kirov director ordered him to stop seeing his French friends, but Rudolf disregarded the warning.

Throughout his years with the Kirov Ballet, Rudolf had been closely monitored due to behavior that was perceived as "anti-Communist." Loyal Communists were expected to repress their individuality and do only what was considered "for the common good."

Rudolf's interest in other cultures and foreign styles of dance was suspect, and he found himself watched by the KGB, the Soviet secret police.

On June 17, 1961, at Le Bourget Airport in Paris, while Rudolf awaited a flight to London, the Kirov director told him of a change in plans. While the rest of the company would finish its tour in London, Rudolf would go to Moscow for a performance at the Kremlin, Russia's governmental headquarters. He knew immediately what the director's words meant: he was being sent back to Russia for insubordination and would likely never again be allowed to leave the country. With a pale face, Rudolf approached a French friend who came to say good-bye, stammering, "That's it. I am finished. Help me or I will kill myself."

Nureyev's fascination with France led to trouble with a Russian government already suspicious of his refusal to participate in its politics

After finding out that he need only approach the French police for help, Rudolf managed to elude a KGB agent and ran into the arms of the police, asking for asylum. Within minutes, Rudolf's life had changed irrevocably. Although he possessed only the clothes on his back and had less than 36 francs (equivalent to about $10) in his pocket, Rudolf was now a free man able to grab any opportunity placed before him. His freedom, however, came at a heartwrenching price: he would never be allowed to return home again.

In his first week of freedom in the West, Rudolf was accepted as a guest performer at the Marquis de Cuevas Ballet Company in Paris. His defection, known in the press as his "leap to freedom," had catapulted him into the international spotlight and immediately presented him with an array of new dance opportunities. Within that year, Rudolf met Danish danseur Erik Bruhn, who became his lover and a lifelong friend. Rudolf also traveled to the United States, making his American debut in a television performance with Native American ballerina Maria Tallchief. But perhaps his most valuable experience was

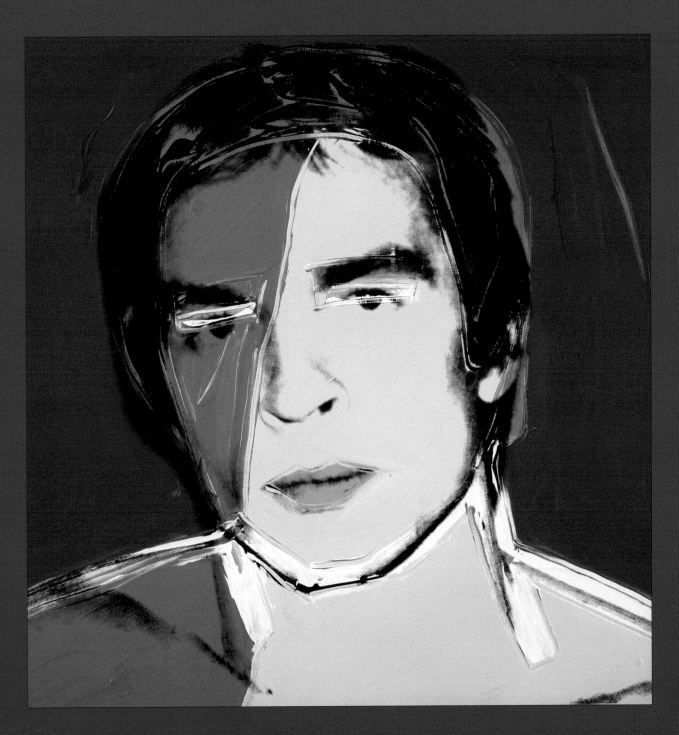

Nureyev was among the famous visitors to the studio of American artist
Andy Warhol, who painted this bold portrait of the dancer around 1975

21

"I truly believe that Rudolf—Rudolf's ability, Rudolf's star power, Rudolf's personality—was instrumental in making ballet the powerful art that it became in the late '60s and the beginning of the '70s."

— *Barbara Horgan, dance administrator for the New York City Ballet*

meeting Margot Fonteyn, the London Royal Ballet's prima ballerina, in the fall of 1961. Having held her position as the company's prima ballerina for more than 20 years, Fonteyn had both the clout and knowledge to lead the young star to new heights.

In the spring of 1962, Rudolf danced with Fonteyn and the Royal Ballet in three landmark performances that established him as one of the most sought-after danseurs in the world. When Rudolf was almost 24 years old, he was made a permanent guest artist with the Royal Ballet, a position he would hold until the age of 38. The guest position

Although Nureyev and Fonteyn each danced with many other partners during their careers, both were most proud of what they achieved together

His never-ending acceptance of roles, including that of the prince in
Sleeping Beauty, helped Nureyev reach a far wider audience than his rivals

allowed him to perform as a principle dancer for the Royal Ballet, one of the world's most

prestigious ballet companies, while also freeing him to pursue other dance opportunities.

Throughout his 20s and 30s, Rudolf accepted almost any dance offer that came his

way. He traveled around the globe, performing as a guest artist for more than 30 of the

world's major dance companies and choreographing about 25 productions. Before the end

of his career, he would dance on every continent except Antarctica. His schedule, whether in London or abroad, was frenetic. If he could schedule performances every day, he would, even if it meant flying to another city or country for just a day or two. During one rehearsal at the Royal Ballet, British ballerina Merle Park said, "Rudolf, you'll kill yourself if you don't slow down." He responded with a smile, "Well, girl, what a better way to die."

On February 21, 1962, Rudolf danced onto the Covent Garden stage in London and started a fire in the world of dance. Some critics praised him, some loathed him, but on the streets of London, everyone spoke the name "Rudolf Nureyev" in hushed, excited tones. His dancing had awakened audiences to a new kind of ballet—a ballet that transformed the traditional dance into an exercise in spontaneity and passion. "Rudimania," the newspapers reported, was sweeping London.

In the fall of 1961, when Rudolf made his London debut, the proudly traditional and often staid ballet world changed. Both onstage and off, Rudolf flaunted his rebellious-

ness and sex appeal, attracting die-hard balletomanes and the curious alike. Recognizing the young star's box office appeal, the director of the London Royal Ballet, Ninette de Vallois, signed him on for three performances of *Giselle* in the spring. And when the refined Margot Fonteyn announced her wish to dance with this young, tempestuous star, people rushed for tickets. The show immediately sold out, and the demand for 70,000 more tickets proved to de Vallois that with Rudolf on the scene, ballet was back in the popular spotlight.

Giselle, one of the classics of romantic ballet, centers on the theme of everlasting love. In Rudolf and Margot's performance, Margot played Giselle, a country maiden who

The Royal Opera House at Covent Garden was the site of Nureyev and Fonteyn's first public performance, which began a 17-year dance partnership

is the object of affection for two men: Hilarion, the village gamekeeper, and Duke Albrecht, who disguises himself as a peasant named Loys. Through the first act, Giselle and Albrecht, played by Rudolf, dance to express their love for one another. Later, when Albrecht feigns love for another and his identity is revealed, the devastated Giselle kills herself. In the last act, a mournful Albrecht clings to Giselle's cross, condemned by spirits to dance to his death. Giselle's spirit then returns to save him, pointing him toward the rising sun and the life that still awaits him.

In his first performance of *Giselle*, Rudolf was stunningly explosive on stage, letting impulses carry him from one movement to another. In a *London Times* review of the performance, the writer described Rudolf's dancing as "ballet acting at its finest." In the

beginning of the ballet, Rudolf's portrayal of Albrecht emphasized the character's human-
ity, showing him as a man confused by his royal status and the pull of his heart. And, after
Giselle commits suicide, Albrecht was drastically transformed. Rudolf wore his anguish
with incredible believability. As the reviewer stated, "His hair [was] disheveled, his
cheeks hollowed, and his eyes [were] burning with a hopeless passion." A primitive, pas-
sionate quality rose to the surface of his dancing, and Margot, like the audience, suc-
cumbed to his passion. Dancing with Rudolf seemed to transform her. The 42-year-old
ballerina's polished demeanor grew more emotional, spontaneous, and alive.

Before his performance of *Giselle*, in previous years of professional dancing, Rudolf
had worked to bring the male dancer's role into the spotlight. Many ballet-goers had

grown accustomed to viewing danseurs as second-class performers, merely assistants to the ballerinas. In *Giselle*, however, his efforts finally received recognition. By establishing his character on equal footing with his female counterpart, Rudolf allowed the audience to experience the true human struggle taking place between Giselle and Albrecht. While some critics were shocked by Rudolf's changes to the choreography, claiming that he drew attention away from the ballerina, ballet aficionados were overjoyed by the emotion and passion injected back into the dance.

At the end of the first *Giselle* performance, the audience's unrelenting applause sent Rudolf and Margot back to the stage for 23 curtain calls. During one of their bows, the ballerina removed a rose from her bouquet and handed it to Rudolf. In a simple motion, Rudolf bowed his head and fell to one knee, looking up at her. He then took the

"I had never seen anything like the way he moved, a man and an animal. It seemed like he jumped into our living room. For boys who grew up on sports, it was like looking at [hockey legend] Wayne Gretzky. You thought, 'That's what I want to do.'"

— *Frank Augustyn, Canada's first world-class danseur, on seeing*

Nureyev on television as a boy

flower and kissed Margot's hand. The audience was so swept up in the dramatic romance of the ballet that it wondered if the dance was still going on.

That night signaled the start of a great partnership, and in only two years, Margot and Rudolf danced in nearly 200 performances together. In the annals of ballet history, they had replaced the famous partnership of Vaslav Nijinsky and Tamara Karsavina. Margot and Rudolf became the ballet world's perfect pair.

33

"Clearly, Nureyev is a very sensational dancer—an extraordinary virtuoso dancer . . . one simply doesn't come across every day. When I first saw him dance, I had the choice of not dancing with him. . . . To dance with Nureyev meant that I would have to make a superhuman effort."

— *Margot Fonteyn, British prima ballerina for the Royal Ballet and a longtime Nureyev dance partner*

Rudolf's partnership with Margot Fonteyn and his contract with the Royal Ballet firmly established his career. From the very start of his career in the West, Rudolf commanded a high salary, typically making $3,000 to $5,000 for a single performance. He appeared on talk shows, late-night television programs, and the children's puppet extravaganza, *The Muppet Show*. He also starred in two unsuccessful Hollywood films: 1977's *Valentino* and 1983's *Exposed*.

With his newfound wealth, Rudolf bought homes, apartments, and villas all over the world, hobnobbing with the rich and famous. With his charming and magnetic—

though moody—personality, the dancer happily fell into his socialite position. While Rudolf formed several long-term relationships with men throughout his lifetime, he expressed his sexual attraction to both men and women through many romantic affairs. No matter what Rudolf was doing or whom he was with, tabloids and newspapers loved to follow him. Whether throwing a drink at someone, smashing expensive china at a party, or simply dancing the night away, Rudolf was someone to watch.

The dancer also remained in the public eye because of his professional experimentation and fearlessness. Aware that most danseurs are considered old at age 30, Rudolf began studying with American modern dance directors Paul Taylor and Martha Graham in the 1970s to broaden his dance possibilities. He also worked as a choreographer and

Nureyev (left) in the 1983 movie Exposed

For his 1982 performance in the controversial Afternoon of a Faun, Nureyev had to convey both strength and innocence as his character matured

Nureyev choreographed the original one-act ballet The Tempest, which he directed members of the Royal Ballet in performing in 1982

producer, staging the Broadway dance hit "Nureyev and Friends," which debuted in 1974 and lasted on and off until 1991. In 1983, at age 45, Rudolf was appointed the artistic director of the Paris Opera Ballet, bringing modern dance principles onto the traditional Paris stage.

During his early years as director, Rudolf began losing weight rapidly and suffering night sweats and fevers. Finally, in 1984, doctors confirmed that the 46-year-old was HIV-

positive and suffering the effects of AIDS. He began taking an experimental drug called HPA-23, which stabilized his health, and continued his ambitious schedule, convinced that he would conquer the disease. Even as he received treatment, Rudolf admitted having the disease only to a small group of friends, and many of them scarcely believed it, since he continued to work with the same energy and determination of his earlier years. But as his dance abilities declined, people began asking with increased frequency when he

would quit. His response was always the same: "For me, dance and life are one. I will dance to the last drop of blood."

The last few years of Rudolf's life were marked by unexpected blessings from his homeland. In 1987, Rudolf was allowed to return to Russia for 48 hours to visit his dying mother. Two years later, he was invited back to Russia for a performance with the Kirov. His dancing was unsteady, and Rudolf knew that the applause was for the dancer he had once been. Still, the long-delayed welcome back to his homeland filled him with joy.

Upon his return from Russia to Paris, Rudolf decided that he didn't have the stam-

ina to dance on stage any longer. He still practiced most days, but it wasn't enough for him; he needed to pour his passion into something else. In 1989, he toured the U.S. as an actor in the Roger and Hammerstein musical *The King and I*, and in 1991, he embarked on a new career as an orchestral conductor. He studied conducting at the Vienna Academy of Music and toured throughout the U.S. and Europe, conducting recitals and ballet concerts.

Rudolf's health, however, increasingly worsened, and he was in and out of the hospital with kidney and heart trouble. His closest friends took turns staying with him at his

From the beginning of his career at the age of 15 until his death at age 54, Nureyev was a revolutionary influence in the world of ballet

Paris apartment, caring for him as he became weaker. In late November 1992, Rudolf entered the hospital for good, no longer able to swallow and needing to be fed intravenously. On the morning of January 6, one of ballet's greatest pioneers passed away.

Friends from all over the world traveled to Paris for the funeral. Flowers and wreaths decorated the steps of the Paris opera house Palais Garnier, where Rudolf had directed and performed. After his funeral, those in attendance drove to the cemetery of Sainte-Genevieve-des-Bois, on the outskirts of Paris. As mourners filed past his casket, some threw flowers; fellow dancers tossed their dance-softened slippers into Rudolf's grave.

"**Dancer, ballet producer, company director, inspirational model, irrestible force and irritant, catalyst, and galvanizer, Rudolf Nureyev remains a point of reference. . . . This was the Nureyev who raised the standard of dancing throughout the world through his own example.**"

— *American dance critic Anna Kisselgoff on Nureyev's 50th birthday*

Nureyev granted many interviews for publication or broadcast, and he wrote an autobiography in 1962. Russian was his first language; although he took English lessons as a student in Leningrad, his grammar was sometimes rough in his early years in the West. In the first excerpt, the 24-year-old recalls how joyful dancing was in his last year of ballet training at the Leningrad Ballet School and touches on differences between Russian and Western ballet. In his specific references to Moscow, he's speaking of his performance at the National Classical Ballet Contest. In the second excerpt, taken from an interview given when he was 32, he shares his perspectives on dance.

The following excerpt is from the 1962 autobiography *Nureyev*.

But how easy, unpredictable, and inspiring dancing seemed to me in those days! I never really knew for sure if I would be able to repeat anything I did but I felt I was really putting the whole of my being into it . . . and that dancing was becoming a life-or-death gamble: win or die. I never knew what would come out. I'm sure that this free and unpredictable quality [communicated] itself to audiences and that they felt they were watching something new; while to me it felt like a miracle.

I don't think I dance as passionately today as I used to then, but though I still have a lot to learn, my technique has become stronger [to compensate]. And as time goes by, dancing becomes less of a gamble, for you know that if the worst happens and inspiration fails you, you can always fall back on your technique.

But at that time, it was a constant surprise and a source of incredible pleasure just to test oneself out, merely because of the uncertainty of the result. Today my approach to dancing is more logical; that almost heart-breaking spontaneity, that kind of suspense I used to feel when dancing, is slowly ebbing away, and with it the violent pleasure I once found in my art. Today, creative joy is a more rational emotion, but on that Moscow evening in June, the feeling of pleasure was wild and violent.

For the first time since I had entered the Leningrad Ballet School I could feel the conspiracy of silence around me breaking up; teachers and model students all came to see me after the performance to offer congratulations. Vassiliev, the best young dancer of the Bolshoi, told me in all sincerity: "You have dazzled and captivated us, Rudolf!" I felt myself turn quite white; no one had ever offered such encouragement. This open admission of my success I found I just couldn't take in my stride; I felt quite shaken inside, so intense was my joy.

Feld, our leading conductor, came specially to offer congratulations for conveying such contrasting moods in a single performance yet still respecting the intrinsic spirit of each ballet.

The fact that Feld had noticed what I had been trying to do made me very happy. As far as I knew, none of the other young dancers of the school approached their work in this way. But to me it seemed the only possible way: that each interpretation must evoke its own special atmosphere, each gesture be colored by its essential, psychologically right meaning.

This I still strongly believe in: the need to invest every part with its own special nuances. A similar combination of steps may occur in several ballets, but every ballet tells a different story through different characters; therefore those steps must be informed by intentions and motives so completely diversified that the public could not possibly mistake one combination for another. This seems to me to call for a research work, conducted by the dancer through his body, rather like the actor may read the same text in several different ways, each time altering thereby the meaning of the words. Through his body, a dancer must give quite different and quite personal readings of ballets, as if they were poems.

Of course this involves a lot of research, but it is endlessly fascinating. It means studying for hours the exact way of placing a shoulder, a chin, or certain stomach muscles. Each part of the body must be studied separately as one might examine the different parts of a machine. Then all those bits of the puzzle must be put together—glued together, one might even say—and submerged into the artist's personal expression. Thus, our dancing, which the public often imagines to be made up of easy, spontaneous movements, is most often the result of days and days of study, of patient long hours spent in front of the mirror severely criticizing oneself for the slightest wrong attitude.

In fact, one must strive to pour more and more of oneself into one's art. If the result is finally understood and acknowledged—then we can have no greater reward.

￼

I explained that my way of dancing needs space for it to become meaningful.

My impulse is toward large, generous steps—a way of dancing which calls for a through-line in space. This is one difference between my style and that of most dancers. I don't think it's even a question of training but of temperament, of a personal approach to dancing. Many dancers tend to contemplate themselves, while I try to give myself to the audience, to fill out the form of the ballet to the full with inner life and feelings. This is the opposite of the kind of narcissistic dancing which allows for contemplation of legs, little hands, and pretty fingers.

Some dancers are at their best on a small stage, which like a jewelry box around them is a perfect décor for miniature steps and movements. Indeed, their work is often as precise and polished as a jeweler's, though with a general lack of scope and generosity.

On small stages one can have no legato, no jumps, no large jetes, no lyricism, no large surging movements; personally it makes me feel like a bird with its wings clipped.

To me a work of art is something alive. To be true to the spirit is, to my mind, much more important than to be what is called correct; for that, in fact, may be less correct, in that it is false to the original idea. In the Covent Garden Giselle, for instance, there are extraneous elements such as the long "Peasant pas de deux" which spoils the dynamic of the first act (incidentally it is by a different composer) and also the long, old-fashioned mime scene by Giselle's mother. You can still see this in some old-fashioned provincial companies in Russia.

I have found this stiff, artificial approach to ballet in a lot of what I have seen in the West. In fact, this is perhaps the big difference between Western ballet and Russian; in Russia the whole approach seems to be more plastic. It starts even in the classroom. Basically, the training is the same; but from the same base you can arrive at quite opposite results. Russian choreography is designed to exploit the Russian style of dancing, with plenty of big jumps and lyrical running and lifting.

Western training produces a better balance, more control, neater feet. But there is a lack of freedom and generosity, of balance and logic in the whole movement.

Western choreography is very much connected to the style of dancing. Of course there are exceptions, such as the wonderful part [ballet choreographer Frederick] Ashton has devised for Margot Fonteyn in Ondine, but on the whole I should say that the lack of great dancers over a long period led to a style where choreographers did not depend on them. Where Western choreography excels is in its general construction, its carpentry. This has obviously been developed to a fine degree.

The more anonymous, team-spirit kind of ballet has also, I think, affected the dancers' approach to their work. They seem able to face any number of performances without worrying. In Russia, where companies are much bigger and full-length ballets are the rule, a soloist appears far less often. With the Kirov my contract stipulated that I should be ready to appear eight times in a month, but actually I never did appear more than three.

This enables a dancer to approach a part deliberately to study and develop it deeply. My ideal is that each performance shall be a first performance, both for myself and for the audience.

The following excerpt is from an interview conducted June 21, 1970, for publication in *The New York Times.*

. . . I really have to dance more often, and so, I travel around. If I don't, I will crumble. Yes, I can see myself as part of the performance company, but only if they give me three to four performances a week. But you see, they cannot. . . . and so, I must dance the classical repertory in other places.

Don't forget that a dancer's life has a span of perhaps twenty or twenty-five years. In that time you have a good period at the beginning, or in the middle, or even at the end. This good period lasts, at best, five to seven years.

It is difficult to spread this very good period evenly, and when you are at your peak, you live off it later on. You live off your fat, so to speak. I feel I am in a very good period now, and I really have to dance nonstop. . . .

First, I must tell you that for me being onstage is really very abnormal, there is something very artificial about it. I must give more, and so, my emotions run very high. Because I feel so alien to the stage, I have a need to be on it more, and more, and more. I find it difficult to get used to, each time. For some dancers, being onstage doesn't matter so much. Their heartbeat doesn't change—nothing really changes. But for me, just standing in the wings, before going on, I am already exhausted, dead. Already my knees are shaking. It's extraordinary how terrified I am. When I have to dance in La Bayadere, for example, a terrible fear goes through me. But when one goes onstage, it should be something extraordinary, it should be like a sacrifice. You cannot go onstage as if you were going to the office. Still, many dancers do this. Yes, they can do wonderful turns, but still, it seems as if they go onstage to do office work.

For myself, the moment I am on the stage things become multiplied and magnified. It's like having an atom reactor inside of me. There is a chain reaction, and, suddenly, my whole body bursts into flames. I suppose if someone were to photograph everything technically, it would probably look all wrong—the line would probably be wrong, etc. But the excitement overflows and spills into the audience, and enflames them.

1938

Rudolf Nureyev is born near Irkutsk in Russia on March 17.

1945

Nureyev sees his first ballet and decides to become a dancer.

1949

Nureyev begins informal ballet training with Anna Udeltsova of Ufa.

1953

The Ufa Opera Ballet accepts Nureyev as a dancer in its corps de ballet.

1955

Nureyev enters the Leningrad Ballet School.

1958

Upon graduation from ballet school, Nureyev takes a soloist position with the Kirov Ballet.

1961

*Nureyev defects from Russia while on tour in Paris; he dances for the
Marquis de Cuevas Ballet and meets Erik Bruhn.*

1962

Nureyev makes his Royal Ballet debut with Margot Fonteyn.

1970

Nureyev dances in his first modern dance performance.

1974

"Nureyev and Friends," the dancer's hit Broadway show, opens in New York.

1983

Nureyev begins working as the ballet director of the Paris Opera Ballet.

1984

Diagnosed as HIV-positive, Nureyev keeps his illness largely a secret for the rest of his life.

1987

Nureyev is allowed into Russia for a brief visit with his mother.

1989

Nureyev tours the United States, performing in the musical The King and I.

1989

Invited back to Russia, Nureyev dances with the Kirov Ballet again.

1991

Nureyev begins a new career as an orchestral conductor.

1992

*La Bayadere is performed at the Paris Opera Ballet; it is the last ballet that
Nureyev choreographs and directs.*

1993

On January 6, Nureyev dies of AIDS in Paris.

AIDS (Acquired Immune Deficiency Syndrome) — *A viral disorder caused by the human immunodeficiency virus (HIV), which attacks the immune system; it is spread through bodily fluids*

Anna Pavlova — *A Russian dancer regarded as the greatest ballerina of the early 1900s because of her exact technique and delicacy on stage*

ballet — *A highly formal and dramatic type of dance recognized by its precise and structured body movements; the name can also refer to a specific dance, such as* Giselle

Communist Party — *A political party that emphasizes equal rights for workers and their families; it lasted in various manifestations in Russia until 1991 and was recognized by many for repressive policies that stifled certain freedoms*

corps de ballet — *The chorus of dancers who all appear together in a ballet performance*

Erik Bruhn — *A Danish dancer who worked as a soloist for the Royal Danish Ballet and toured the world as a guest artist and director in the mid- to late-1900s*

George Balanchine — *A Russian ballet dancer and choreographer who served as ballet director for the New York Metropolitan Opera House and choreographer for the New York City Ballet in the late 1900s*

Kirov Ballet — *A Russian ballet company based in Leningrad; considered one of the best dance companies in Europe, the Kirov was founded in 1738 as the Imperial Russian Ballet*

Margot Fonteyn — *A British ballerina who served as the Royal Ballet's prima ballerina from the 1930s to the '60s and was recognized for her great versatility*

modern dance — *An experimental dance developed in the United States and Germany in the 20th century; it emphasizes free movement of the body rather than the rigid body positions of ballet*

The Royal Ballet — *England's best-known ballet company, located in London; it was originally founded as the Vic-Wells Ballet in 1926*

Russia — *From 1922 to 1991, the official name for Russia was the Union of Soviet Socialist Republics, or the USSR; the names Russia, USSR, and Soviet Union were all used interchangeably*

Tamara Karsavina — *A Russian prima ballerina known for her partnership with Vaslav Nijinsky in the early 1900s*

Vaslav Nijinsky — *A Russian ballet dancer and choreographer known for his powerful, erotic style on stage; he was hailed by many as the best danseur of the 20th century*